Copyright 2021

ISBN: 9780578967189

First paperback edition December 15, 2021

Book design by Cris Cawthon

Thank you

I would like to thank the following people Laura Ashby, Stephen Nail, Jan Monken-Atchison, and Elizabeth Wallace. This book would not have been possible without your contribution.

Thank you also for those who helped with edit suggestions. Carol McCrary, Kathy Eifert, and Peggy Bennett.

Thank you also to all those who believed in me and rooted me on to complete this book.

Without you, this book would not have been possible.

Introduction

Where do we turn when life hands us a river of tears; a sickness incurable; a family torn apart; or defeat at its worst?

Well, I hope and pray that you will find something in this book that encourages you to strive forward. Maybe a verse that speaks volumes to your current situation, or a personal experience of mine that shows you, you are not alone.

I must add that this book alone is not the answer to the above questions. Spending time with God and His Word is the solution to the problems we often face today. Prayer is a necessity in your Christian life. Without it, we lose the closeness we need with God.

I hope you enjoy this book and share it with others. My prayer is that you find comfort from the good Lord above and always remember that you are not alone. He is with you.

Be encouraged!

Chapter

In memory of my Grandma

My Grandma Willa Cawthon died December 15, 2012. Every memory of her always brings a smile to my face.

Her teachings were always about the Love of God and living a life that's pleasing to Him. She is sadly missed by so many, and it is only fitting of me to remember her by the word she used every time we ended our phone call, "Be encouraged".

I pray you find peace and understanding in your walk with the Lord, and that His light will continue to shine through you as you share His truth, love, and mercy with those around you. God Bless!

Submitted by L. Rohner

Chapter 1

Disciplining Ourselves Spiritually

Recently, at church, we had a guest speaker. The lesson he shared with us had many good and thoughtful points... the kind that makes you look at your life and change some things.

The definition of discipline is: control gained by enforcing obedience or order. The definition of spirituality is: concerned with religious values. If we put the two together, we come up with; continue to be concerned about the practice of training our spiritual life.

If we are concerned about our spiritual life, growth, and our example to others, then we have to continue to practice training ourselves in the Word.

The Sunday lesson was about feeding on the knowledge of God's Word.

The speaker shared that physical exercise is important but that our spiritual life is more important.

He went on to add that if we have God's Word in our life, it would help us to resist temptation. 2 Peter 1:3 reads: "His divine power has given us everything we need for a godly life through our knowledge of him who called us by his own glory and goodness."

When we put our all into studying God's Word like the Bereans in the Bible, then our life will show it.

The Bereans searched the scripture daily. Acts 17:11 reads: "Now the Berean Jews were of more noble character than those in Thessalonica, for they received the message with great eagerness and examined the scriptures every day to see if what Paul said was true."

We may have good intentions to wake up and start the day with God, but then we let the cares of this world get in our way.

I know time is limited when the demands of this world constantly need our attention. Some days it seems there are not enough hours in the day. No matter what, we must stop to make time.

The speaker Sunday said, "Lift the spiritual weights by reading God's Word." The speaker described the Bible as, "the bread of life and sweeter than honey." Psalm 34:9 reads: "Taste and see that the LORD is good; blessed is the one who takes refuge in him."

What more could we as Christians want than to be pleasing in the sight of God? 2 Corinthians 5:20 reads: "we are ambassadors to Christ." I want to also encourage you to read 2 Corinthians 5:11-21.

The Webster's dictionary defines ambassador as: "an authorized representative or messenger." Sisters and Brothers in Christ, we have an obligation to be messengers.

It is our responsibility to read God's Word, live God's Word, and share God's Word.

The speaker had another great point: "We have to be willing to cut things out of our life in order to control our desires."

 He went on to say, we need to be eating the right spiritual diet, exercising the right spiritual exercise, and setting the right spiritual goals.

Dear heavenly Father, help me to be mindful of my use of time, help me always to put you first. I pray that each person who reads this will be encouraged. Lord, my heart shouts with joy, for I am confident of your love and sacrifice for me. Continue to help me to be a witness to others and pleasing in your sight. Amen

(Original prayer by Cris Cawthon)

Reflections

_____

_____

_____

_____

_____

_____

_____

_____

_____

_____

_____

_____

_____

_____

_____

_____

Chapter 2

Grace and Glory

Psalm 84:11 reads: "For the Lord God is a sun and shield: the LORD will give grace and glory: no good thing will he withhold from them that walk uprightly."

Merriam Webster dictionary defines grace as "unmerited divine assistance given to humans for their regeneration or sanctification and a virtue coming from God: a state of sanctification enjoyed through divine assistance. Glory is: "praise, honor, or distinction extended by common consent: worshipful praise, honor, and thanksgiving; giving glory to God."

Grace is such a beautiful word. I remember when they use to call my late Grandma Willa, Mother Grace.

She had such poise and sweetness. Her attitude was meek, humble, and full of eagerness to serve the Lord.

I would only hope that I have an ounce in me of who she was.

Although I admired her Christ-like mannerisms, her real grace came from the gift God gave us all. Ephesians 2:8 reads: "For it is by grace you have been saved, through faith--and this is not from yourselves, it is the gift of God."

When you think of a gift, what comes to mind? Is it something you give someone for their birthday, Christmas, or just because. A gift should be something you freely give with no strings attached.

God gave his son as a gift. We could never give anyone else a gift that compares to this. Though this gift was not given to us wrapped in pretty paper or with a bow, its unconditional value saw something that was worth saving us. This gift hung on a cross with a crown of thorns pressed firmly into His head. This gift, shed blood though he was innocent. This gift had a spear pushed into his side and still uttered the words, "forgive them for they know not what they do." Luke 23:34. That is grace!

If we do not see this gift as our salvation and eternal home in Heaven, then we are to blame. God's Word is available to all. It is up to us to pick it up and study it.

2 Corinthians 12:8-9 reads: "Three times I pleaded with the Lord to take it away from me but he said to me, 'My grace is sufficient for you, for my power is made perfect in weakness.'" Therefore, I will boast all the more gladly about my weaknesses, so that Christ's power may rest on me."

Wow, we are supposed to boast in our weakness. Does this even sound like something one could do after losing a job or finding out they are sick? It's hard to feel any strength when faced with trials, but be sure of this, Christ's power will rest on you. This assurance stirs a song in my soul, "Glory, Glory, and Hallelujah! Since I laid my burdens down! Glory, Glory, and Hallelujah! Since I laid my burdens down! I feel so much better, so much better since I laid my burdens down!"

It reads in Romans 8:18-19: "I consider that our present sufferings are not worth comparing with the glory that will be revealed in us. For the creation waits in eager expectation for the children of God to be revealed."

Glory and splendor awaits for those who are children of God. We should get excited about this.

All of our sufferings here on earth are temporary. It may seem like the end of the world sometimes, but hang in there and look forward to that heavenly home.

I have had my share of unhappy circumstances and some unique, unsolved, medical problems, but my faith has kept me strong. There are nights that I have cried myself to sleep in pain, or have been so exhausted from multiple surgeries, that I wanted to wake up in glory the next day. God heard my cries and His Word bought me comfort

Proverbs 24:19 reads: "do not fret." As easy as it sounds, it is often the hardest thing to do.

Having disagreements between friends, do not fret. Is someone at work causing you problems, do not fret?

Do you have family members working against you, do not fret? Where does fretting get you? Nowhere except worried with more wrinkles and possibly ulcers. If we trust in the Lord, He will provide. Turn your fret into prayers!

Dear Heavenly Father, thank you for the Grace that was shown to us through your Son's death. Thank you for Your Word and how it uplifts us through our trials. Father, there are so many hurting, so many that will not accept your grace. Help me, Father, to not hinder or be an obstacle in anyone's way, but to encourage, uplift and share the glory that is heaven-bound. Father, I have suffered so much, but still, you carry me through. Thank you for allowing me to be able to express myself through writing, so that others may be encouraged. Father, I am so excited about what awaits me and I know everything here is temporary. Suffering will come but my light will continue to shine for you. In Jesus Christ Name

Amen!

Original prayer by (Cris Cawthon)

Reflections

_____
_____
_____
_____
_____
_____
_____
_____
_____
_____
_____
_____
_____
_____
_____
_____
_____

Chapter 3

How Sure Are You

When it comes to your faith, how sure are you? Are you sure that no matter what obstacles, trials, or heartaches you face, your faith will remain strong? What if your faith was tested... are you 100 percent sure that you could pass that test without hesitation?

One of the characteristics of being a Christian is to be imitators of Christ. It does not mean we will be perfect, but we do need to strive to be better Christians. Are you willing to commit to serving God daily?

If you wake up each morning with an attitude that no matter what that day brings, you will live a life that is pleasing in God's eyes, then I think it will help you to be more conscious of the places you go, the people you hang out with, and the choice of words you use.

It is a work in progress to be a faithful Christian. Some people think its easy peasy; and that once you are baptized for the remission of your sins, you will then be free from sin and no longer tempted by the world.

This belief is false on every level. Luke 9:23-24 reads: He was saying to them all, "If anyone wishes to come after Me, he must deny himself, and take up his cross daily and follow Me. ""For whoever wishes to save his life will lose it, but whoever loses his life for My sake, he is the one who will save it."

You have to work at it and study God's Word so that you can become stronger to resist the temptations and the sinful entertainment in this world.

There are many individuals in the Bible that were tested just to see how committed they were to serving God.

How sure do you think Peter was? Well, I am sure he was confident at the beginning of his walk with Christ and he believed he would always remain faithful.

Maybe you, or someone you know, started out full of that zeal and confidence and now you feel like it's not as important. Do not lose that.

Matthew 26:35 reads: "But Peter declared, "Even if I have to die with you, I will never disown you." And all the other disciples said the same.

It sounds like he was sure at the time, no matter what, he would even go as far as dying with Christ. That's true commitment.

If you read on further in Matthew 26:69-75, you will see that Peter was approached three different times, and was asked if he was the one with Jesus Christ.

Each time he denied he even knew him. Wow! Jesus had told Peter that he would deny him three times before the rooster crowed and sure enough, after the rooster crowed, Peter remembered the words of Jesus and he wept. Do you think he wept because he realized he failed Jesus?

Our intentions as a Christian may begin like Peters, we want to stand up for Jesus, tell others about Jesus, and reveal Him in our daily lives. This is how it should be, but have you grown weary and been caught off guard? Have you been faced with a tough decision that hinders your walk with Christ, or have you denied Him already? How sure are you in serving the Lord no matter the outcome?

It is not always easy, but possible. The Bible tells of another man, but this one showed how possible it was to live life with faith.

Job had everything taken from him; from his family to his livestock, but he remained faithful. At one point, even his wife encouraged him to turn from God.

In Job 2:9, Job's wife said to him, "Are you still maintaining your integrity? Curse God and die!"

Even those we care about can be an obstacle in our walk with the Lord. Job suffered greatly, but he did not turn his back on his commitment to serve God.

Today, I challenge you to separate yourself from anything that may be hindering you from giving your all to Christ.

Cling to 1 Corinthians 16:13: "be on your guard; stand firm in the faith; be courageous; be strong."

Reflections

_____

_____

_____

_____

_____

_____

_____

_____

_____

_____

_____

_____

_____

_____

_____

_____

_____

_____

Chapter 4

Jesus or Junk

Have you ever wondered why your favorite color is your favorite color? What about why you like a certain number better than you like the other?

My favorite color is yellow and my favorite number is five. Why? Well yellow is bright like the sun. The color yellow is illuminating and cheerful. Yellow is bold! I like the number five because my birthday is the fifth month of the year. No deep thought here, just a simple answer.

I suppose you thought I was going to dig deeper into some scientific reasoning or psychological theory about how and why those mean something. Nope! Really, it is my choice to like what I like without reasoning.

Life is full of many things that mean a lot to us. Some are with reasoning, and some, just because.
Do you have things in your life that have meaning?

Do they have a purpose? Do you have joy from them? Is there value in them? Do they have worth? Do they bring you contentment? Whatever your reason is for liking the things you like, and placing them first in your life, it is WRONG. Yes, I said it. Wrong!

I have a lot of material things that I like and value. I have things that make me smile, things that comfort me, things that are full of knowledge (books), and things that makes me happy when I see them.

I will say this, I do not, and will not place these things before Jesus. I wrote a blog not long ago, and in that blog, I made this statement, Jesus could have called down 10, 000 angels to rescue Himself. He put us first so why not put Him first.

If you have to think about what's more important when I ask this question, Jesus, or junk, then you have some serious soul searching to do.

So, which is it, Jesus, or junk? Time is ticking, are you still thinking about this?

Let me help you by sharing the verse in Matthew 6:19-20: "Do not store up for yourselves treasures on earth, where moths and vermin destroy, and where thieves break in and steal. But store up for yourselves treasures in heaven, where moths and vermin do not destroy, and where thieves do not break in and steal. For where your treasure is, there your heart will be also."

You see, where your treasures are, there your heart will also be. My treasures are being stored in heaven.

Yes, no doubt, I like my things and I worked hard for everything thing that I have, but I cannot take them with me after this life.

In Matthew 19:21 it reads: "Jesus answered, "If you want to be perfect, go, sell your possessions and give to the poor, and you will have treasure in heaven. Then come, follow me."

Wow! Perfect! Like in the lyrics from the song, "Perfect Submission." [All is at rest I in my Savior am happy and blessed, watching and waiting, looking above filled with His goodness, lost in His love].

We know that none of us is perfect, but would you say that your life is committed to serving the Lord? Are you ready and willing to surrender your all to the Lord?

In the Bible, a couple pretended to be committed. They wanted to do well and give but in spite of the good came deception. They lied about giving their all. Are you pretending to give to the lord by showing up in church on Sunday but then willfully sinning the other days?

It reads in Acts 5:1-3, "Now a man named Ananias, together with his wife Sapphira, also sold a piece of property. With his wife's full knowledge, he kept back part of the money for himself, but brought the rest and put it at the apostles' feet." Then Peter said, "Ananias, how is it that Satan has so filled your heart that you have lied to the Holy Spirit and have kept for yourself some of the money you received for the land?"

In life, I want to be faithful and complete every day. Can you say the same for your life?

Are your children's sports and activities more important than living a life that's pleasing to God? Do you like the "credit card" more than you do serving God and giving some of what you have to further the kingdom? Do you stay at home Sunday morning just because your spouse does?

If the hair on your arms does not stand up and your heart is not pricked, then you are more calloused than you should be. Christ church was built upon a rock: a firm, solid foundation. Is your heart so hard and callous that it is beyond smoothing out and transforming back to loving Christ first? It can be done if you desire it.

Stop going through life putting junk before Jesus. Stop thinking that maybe tomorrow I will be a better Christian or next Sunday I will try and attend worship service.

Stop spitting in Jesus' face and get your life together. If you do not think that serving Him is important and that what he did for you on that cross was evidence of His love, then you are no different from those on the ground shouting out, "Crucify Him." If this does not give you goosebumps or prick your heart, then I am afraid even a defibrillator will not revive you. Instead of the medical term, "code blue," it would be "code you need Jesus."

Take time right now and reflect on what Jesus did for us. Go ahead, stop reading for a moment, and close your eyes. (Pause)

If you imagined what I did, isn't it an honor to serve someone who loves us without conditions and limitations? When I closed my eyes, this is what I envisioned. Jesus was walking down the road spreading encouragement to all those He met. He stooped down to heal those with unimaginable diseases.

Everywhere He walked people flocked to Him. Now picture this; Jesus is walking to the garden to pray. As He prays, He feels a little bit of grief because of what He knows is coming. After He prayed, He met with the disciples.

They ate and had a great fellowship. Later some men had come to get Jesus. The disciples were concerned but Jesus went willingly.

The people around Him were shouting and their faces were overcome with anger. Jesus began to grow weary and wanted nothing more than His present situation to pass.

Jesus now hangs on a cross with nails driven through His hands and feet.

He listens to the people and His heart grieves. They place a crown of thorns on His head. The men now drive a spear into His side and He is bleeding profusely. I know He must be in agony and pain. It is not His will but His Fathers will because it is all for a greater purpose.

Toward the final hours, Jesus still finds it in His heart to forgive the people as he utters the words, "forgive them for they know not what they do."

We could never place ourselves in Jesus' shoes, but can you imagine if it were you for the sake of your enemies to give your life in such a way?

What is more important to you, Jesus or junk?

Reflections

_____

_____

_____

_____

_____

_____

_____

_____

_____

_____

_____

_____

_____

_____

_____

_____

_____

Chapter 5

Self-Examine

Hey you, yes, the one reading this, are you ready to learn about self-examination?

If you are, please continue. I promise you will not regret it. The meaning of self-examine according to Webster's dictionary is the study of one's own behavior and motivations. The keywords are **study**, **behavior**, and **motivations**.

When you evaluate your behavior, are the results shocking? When you evaluate yourself, are you motivated to do anything or just get by on a whim? How do you behave when faced with a crisis?

 You may think your life is A-OK and you may feel that after you self-examine, everything is just how it should be.

You see no reason to change anything about your life.

I will tell you this as a fact; with an attitude like that, it sends a red flag to others that you really are a prideful person.

Throughout many years of my life, I have learned that there is always room for improvement.

No matter how you view who you are, it will come out in your actions. People are watching and what they see often does not match who we make ourselves out to be. There are many people that hide behind social media.

For some reason it gratifies them to portray a perfect life, when in reality they are falling apart.

I want you to take a moment and self-examine your life. **GET REAL** about who you are.

If your life is full of unhappiness, feelings of emptiness, and exhaustion from pretending everything is ok, then you need intervention. Do not hide behind a fake life just to please others.

When circumstances in life weigh you down, I know it is hard to look at anything in life with a positive attitude. I know sometimes that it is hard to get excited about anything in your life because it all seems like a disappointment.

I was not always happy about who I was. Yes, depression consumed most of my life. At one time during a dark period in my life, I felt like my life was worthless. There were times I didn't want to live.

Other people saw me in a different light. They saw more of a laid back, quiet, and loving person. Yes, I was also all of that, but I was also drowning in my own misery. I still had faith in God. I knew there was a stronger foundation out there than what I was standing on.

When I reached out to God's inspired Word with commitment, it was then that I was able to see my worth.

Self-denial caused me to self-examine myself with blinders. There were times in which I felt that if I did not exist, then life would have been much better for others.

When I finally saw a little good in myself, I stopped letting my circumstances define who I am.

I stopped letting depression rob me of what I was capable of doing. Being stuck in a rut is exhausting.

A friend said to me, that doing the same thing is insanity. It is similar to the phrase, do the same thing, the same way and you will always get the same results.

If you feel like a "nobody" all the time, you will act and behave like a nobody. Open your eyes and heart; if you want a better life, then you will have to change some things. Maybe you have pretended things were "ok" for way too long, it has begun to affect your motivation to do something about it.

Examine yourself and find your true self!

Stop looking more at the self-pride and be real, unique, and ready to do great things. The Bible reads in Proverbs 16:18: "Pride goes before destruction, "a haughty spirit before a fall."

As a Christian, I am self-examining in a broader aspect. It is more than just emotionally important but spiritually important.

If I profess to bear the name, Christian, then how I behave should reflect that.

If there is any part of my outward life that does not show evidence of that, then how can I be genuine inside? I know the Lord looks at my heart and that is more of a reason to be pure and devoted to serving Christ.

Anyone can profess that they are a Christian, but when you self-examine, the truth is revealed.

This Bible verse comes to mind, 2 Corinthians 13:5: "Examine yourselves as to whether you are in the faith. Test yourselves. Do you not know yourselves that Jesus Christ is in you? —unless indeed you are disqualified."

We are not perfect human beings, but we do have to be serious about our service to God.

If you have been going with the flow and telling yourself that you check out pretty good compared to someone else, then you need to re-examine that attitude.

It is about who **YOU** are. We do not get to heaven flying on the wings of someone else's faith.

Today, get yourself together before you reach the point of self-destruction. Get your life in order and prioritize what is important.

It took me years to be able to say this, "I am happy about who I am." I am also forever grateful for the unconditional love of Christ.

There is always need for improvement, not just this temple, but also how I prioritize my study in God's Word. Each day should start with loving God with ALL of me. Are you able to self-examine with a Christ-like attitude, and love Him with all your heart?

The Bible reads in Mark 12:30-31: "Love the Lord your God with all your heart and with all your soul and with your entire mind and with all your strength."

The second is this: "Love your neighbor as yourself. There is no commandment greater than these."

Are you able to love your neighbor if you do not even love yourself? That would be a difficult one.

Self-examine!

Reflections

_____

_____

_____

_____

_____

_____

_____

_____

_____

_____

_____

_____

_____

_____

_____

_____

_____

SUBMITTED BY J. ROHNER

Chapter 6

Spending time with God

When you wake up in the morning, your first words should be "Thank you God for blessing me with another day."

When I wake up in the morning, I am eager to start the day. It does not always turn out the way I want it to, but with a positive attitude and putting the Lord first in my life, I plan for it to be a better day than it could have been if I got up with a negative attitude.

One morning I called my friend before I left the house and when she answered, she seemed quieter than she normally was. I asked her if she wanted the mashed potatoes that I had made. Her reply was: "No."

A little later, after we had hung up, I received a text from her. This was her reply, "Be safe, I was having my devotion when you called." I texted back and said,

"Well that's way more important than those mashed potatoes."

If we begin our day with God in prayer, in the Word, and devotion, then I am certain of this, it will make a big difference in our day.

The situations we encounter may not always be wonderful, but because we took time with God; the way we approach a situation can have a better outcome.
We have to remember what's more important in our lives.
We have to remember that the word was put there for us; to give us answers and instructions on how to live our daily lives.

The Bible is full of compiled scriptures that are inspired by God and given to us through men.

We need to be serious in our relationship with God. We cannot take one part of the verse as truth, and the other part questionable just because it does not apply to our life. Every verse in the Bible is sound doctrine.

In 1 Corinthians 14:33, it reads, "For God is not the author of confusion, but of peace, as in all churches of the saints." He did not put one verse one place, and chapters later, it contradict themselves. No, it all makes sense. We just have to open our hearts and put away our selfish, stubborn, and prideful attitudes.

If you think your life is just fine and only some of the Bible applies to you, then you have been listening to the wrong person and have been misled and misguided. Every part of the Bible matters!

There are times in my life when I did not understand many things. I was sad about many things growing up. Even though I was brought up going to worship services, I was still confused.

It was only when I began to search the Word for myself that I grasped a better understanding. The Bible is written for all people. I stopped feeling like the joy I saw in others was not acceptable for me to have.

I remember my Grandma used to say that one could not take the faith that others have; they have to get it on their own. That always stuck with me. I knew her to be a very strong, faithful person but no matter how much time I spent with her, her faith alone was not going to be enough for me or get me to heaven.

Growing to know more about God, I continued to go to church. I felt such a closeness to God through studying His inspired Word.

I was beginning to understand it more and more. I felt that being a true, God-fearing Christian was such a joyous feeling. No one could take that from me.
 It took work on my part to get to where I am. Yes, work. I had to stay committed, consistent and humble myself many times. It is hard to stay consistent with all the things going on in this world.

There is so much entertainment out there that can distract us. My advice is, never put God on the back burner.

I know it is easy to get side tracked when we are involved with so many other things. Just do not forget to pick up the Bible and study it. That is why I said before, it takes work.

We must remember that we are not of this world, so we need to be mindful of the greater sacrifice and do our part to be better Christians.

1 John 2:15-17 reads: "Do not love the world or the things in the world. If anyone loves the world, the love of the Father is not in him." For all that is in the world—the lust of the flesh, the lust of the eyes, and the pride of life—is not of the Father but is of the world. And the world is passing away, and the lust of it; but he who does the will of God abides forever."

There are things in this world that are going to come up against us and try to trip us up. There are times in which our joy may be challenged, our peace disrupted and our time with the Lord is less and less. Stay prayerful!

It reads in 1 Thessalonians 5:16-18" "Rejoice always, pray without ceasing, in everything give thanks; for this is the will of God in Christ Jesus for you."

If we do not remain consistent, then we become vulnerable to temptation.

Going back to my friend that was doing her devotion, those potatoes did not matter to her at the time and that was ok. We have to spend time with God so that we are better prepared to face whatever is thrown at us.

Where are you in your life right now? Are you grabbing for those potatoes and neglecting time with God? Are you seeking entertainment in this world and neglecting time with God?

I am not saying it is going to be easy to keep from getting distracted and tempted. Jesus himself was tempted. In Matthew 4:1-11 it reads: "Then Jesus was led up by the Spirit into the wilderness to be tempted by the devil."

In addition, when He had fasted forty days and forty nights, afterward He was hungry. Now when the tempter came to Him, he said, "If you are the Son of God, command that these stones become bread. "But He answered and said, "It is written, 'Man shall not live by bread alone, but by every word that proceeds from the mouth of God.'

"Then the devil took Him up into the holy city, set Him on the pinnacle of the temple, and said to Him, "If you are the Son of God, throw yourself down.

For it is written: "He shall give His angels charge over you,' and, 'in their hands they shall bear you up, lest you dash your foot against a stone.'" Jesus said to him, "It is written again, 'you shall not tempt the Lord your God.' Again, the devil took Him up on an exceedingly high mountain, and showed Him all the kingdoms of the world and their glory and he said to Him, "All these things I will give you if you will fall down and worship me." Then Jesus said to him, "Away with you, Satan! For it is written, 'You shall worship the Lord your God, and Him only you shall serve.' Then the devil left Him, and behold, angels came and ministered to Him."

It may be challenging to have your mind right and ready to serve God, but it means you will have to sort through what is important in your life.

You may have heard the phrase: "We fall short." Yes, we are imperfect people, but it does not mean we have to close our Bible, stop our devotion time, stop going to worship service and neglect spending time with God.

There were many martyrs in the Bible that sacrificed their lives for God. Stephen was one of them.

He was full of wisdom and allowed the Holy Spirit to work through him. He was later stoned to death, as written in Acts 8:54.

Would you be willing to stand boldly for God?

Many of us would answer yes. Some will stand up and proclaim His name, until they are faced with temptation.

Peter was confident that he would not deny Jesus. I believe in his heart he wanted to honor Jesus with every ounce of himself. Peter was 100% sure at the time that he was not going to turn his back on Jesus. That is until life situations happened and the test of faith was at hand, read Matthew 26: 60-75.

Temptation is out there. We have to stay faithful in prayer and continue to rely on God's Word.

When you wake up, repeat this: "I will serve the Lord this day." Repeat this: "In times of trouble I will serve the Lord even through my heartache and pain. I will serve the Lord when I face misunderstanding and persecution. I will serve the Lord through disappointments and rejections. I will serve the Lord through it all."

Spending time with God is a genuine way to have a relationship with Him. I know life is tough, trust me, I can attest to it considering the life I have lived. Whining about it does nothing. I have to try daily to lay my burdens down at the foot of the cross and continue to shine for Jesus.

When we are in worship, we cannot be bright lights sitting on a pew among fellow brothers and sisters in Christ, and then go into the world and act like hypocrites.

Come on people, smile at others and share God's Word and love for them. Let your light shine if you want to help win souls for the Kingdom of God.

Matthew 5:14-16 reads: "You are the light of the world. A city that is set on a hill cannot be hidden. Nor do they light a lamp and put it under a basket, but on a lampstand, and it gives light to all who are in the house.

"Let your light so shine before men, that they may see your good works and glorify your Father in heaven. Amen!"

Reflections

_____

_____

_____

_____

_____

_____

_____

_____

_____

_____

_____

_____

_____

_____

_____

_____

_____

Chapter 7

The Simple Life

"Therefore, I tell you, do not worry about your life, what you will eat or drink; or about your body, what you will wear. Is not life more important than food, and the body more important than clothes? Look at the birds of the air; they do not sow or reap or store away in barns, and yet your heavenly Father feeds them. Are you not much more valuable than they" Matthew 6:27 reads, who of you by worrying can add a single hour to his life?"

I have always been fascinated with the Amish way of life ever since I can remember.

The most intriguing part about them is their simple way of life. Wouldn't it be great if we could slow our life down a little?

If you wrote down a list of things you had to fit in your agenda today, I'm sure it over exceeds the amount of time you have to do it all.

The Amish have busy lives that are full of hard labor, but they still keep it simple and rely on God to provide.

The verse above says not to worry about what we will wear. Yes, it's nice to look neat and clean, but should we spend so much time dwelling on those things to the point of worshipping our appearance more?

When I visited the Amish community in Arthur, IL, it was almost as if I had been teleported into another world. Life was slower there. I was greeted with warm, friendly smiles. Their clothing was plain and alike. Their buggies were so slow; no one was in a hurry. The sound of the horse hooves hitting the pavement was so relaxing. Clippty-clop clippty-clop.

How can we simplify our lives like those in the Amish community? Simple!

Learn to prioritize your "to do" list so that you don't get overwhelmed and frustrated.

One of the main points I'm driving at, is to simplify your life from earthly things and focus on the Lord's promises to provide for you.

I'm not excluding myself, I too need to learn to pace myself and do what's capable within my means.

1 Thessalonians 4:11 reads, "Make it your ambition to lead a quiet life, to mind your own business and to work with your hands, just as we told you, so that your daily life may win the respect of outsiders and so that you will not be dependent on anybody."

A quiet life opens doors for quiet time with the Lord. If you are missing that, then you need to re-evaluate what is more important in your daily life.

Most of us have more than we can imagine. Our homes are by far simple. I would say mine is busy with lots of stuff.

If I let stuff take priority over my walk with the Lord, then I am choosing it over Him.

Do not get me wrong, I like my stuff, but not more than my duty to serve and praise God. With that said, it is also my duty as a professing Christian to share God's Word with others.

If we continue to walk with the Lord and let our ways be pleasing in His sight, we will find that peace that I'm sure the Amish people feel.

Take a moment and say a prayer for the Lord to help you prioritize things in your life. Humbly ask him to give you a quieter life.

Today I challenge you to take notice of the simple things around you.

The birds chirping, the flower blossoms, the bees buzzing, the hoot howl, and whatever else brings an ounce of peace your way. I will leave you with this verse, "Be still and know that I am God" Psalm 46:10.

Reflections

Chapter 8

Standing on the promises

"Standing on the promises of Christ my King, through eternal ages let His praises ring, Glory in the highest; I will shout and sing, standing on the promises of God. Standing, standing, standing on his promises."

Composer Russell Kelso Carter wrote this hymn in 1849. The hymn reflects his own personal experience when near death; he battled a heart disease at the age of 30. The words are a testament to his faith.

Connie Ruth Christiansen writes, "He knelt and made a promise that healing or not, his life was finally and forever, consecrated to the service of the Lord." Christiansen said it was then; that he begins to lean on the promises that he found in the Bible.

So often, we face trials and pray to God trusting his answer will always be in our favor. I mean after all; he is a loving God, right?

Well, it doesn't always work that way. Yes, Russell Carter lived another 49 years, but does this mean he prayed harder than anyone else, or lived a more faithful life than anyone else? No, it just wasn't his time to go.

When we pray asking God to help us through whatever we are going through, we must remember to pray knowing that all will be done in HIS will.

Do you recall the verse in 1 John 5:14-15? It reads: "This is the confidence we have in approaching God: that if we ask anything according to his will, he hears us. And if we know that he hears us— whatever we ask — we know that we have what we asked of him."

I want a brand-new car that will last me a long time. I have prayed for that, believed it, and still no new car.
Does this mean 1 John 5:14-15 isn't true? If I ask for something,

should get it, right? Let me rephrase this to give you a better understanding of where I'm going with this.

have prayed for something that I may or may not really need at this time but God has heard my prayer and when and if it is to happen for me, it will happen in His time and will.

Sometimes prayers just aren't answered the way we want them too.

There is so much controversy over why God answers one prayer and doesn't the other. Well, my response to this is; our trust should always remain in the Lord no matter how our prayers are answered. I pray not my will but HIS.

There are so many lessons we will learn through our trials. It isn't FAIR how things happen, but God has a plan for everything and his word is full of promises if we keep the faith.

A friend of mine has a note on her refrigerator that once hung in her classroom. It said, "Fair is a place you go in the summer time to get a corndog."

I thought that was the funniest quote and a good way to say, nothing in life is always fair.

I've endured countless traumas in my life that were not fair, but I had to learn to cling to God.

My sister was brutally murdered at the age of 33, shot three times. The last bullet to the head killed her. She was also thrown out of the vehicle and onto a main highway. What a Horrific crime!

I can spend countless hours asking God why. I can spend the rest of my days being angry and bitter. I should be angry, right? After all, that was my big sister. It's my choice to be angry, but what would it benefit me or those around me?

As sorrowful as it may have been for me and my family, it is not for me to question why it happened to her and not someone else.

I can only imagine 2,000 years ago that Mary had also experienced pain so devastating. She watched her son beaten and hung on a cross for a sin he did not commit.

Jesus flesh was torn apart and blood profusely flowing down. Oh, what agony. I can only imagine how hard this was for Mary to watch.

Unlike my sister; Jesus could have ended this by calling down 10, 000 angles. Matthew 26:53 reads: "Do you think I cannot call on my Father, and he will at once put at my disposal more than twelve legions of angels? But how then would the Scriptures be fulfilled that say it must happen in this way?" This verse gives me chills. In a good way of course. The awesome power of God!

Maybe you are wondering Why Jesus didn't call on the father. Well, there was a greater purpose for you and me.

A bigger plan!

We could spend countless hours on end trying to figure out the reason for the losses we see, the destruction around us, the pain, the violence, the hatred, and the racism. It grieves my heart to even watch the news, but what can I do about all of the above?

We can read books by Nostradamus who is supposed to be able to foresee the future, but of course, his predictions never came true.

We can read books about Charles Darwin who believed in evolution.

His 1859 book, Origin of Species, talks about the process by which organisms change over time because of changes inheritable physical or behavioral traits. This is Nonsense!

Let's stop entertaining these theories, as Christians take a stand, and teach the truth. All of the above are simply not God's plan. We must continue to share with others the one book that we can pick up and know the outcome.

The Bible!

If we stand on His promises, we will not only find strength through our trials but also hope in knowing something better is coming.

Do I miss my sister even though I know there is a scripture that says in (Ecclesiastes 3:2), "that there is a time to be born and a time to die? Yes, I miss my sister daily."

Do I know for sure that she will make it to that wonderful place called heaven? I don't know.

I may not understand the plan for my life but I know God's promises if I remain faithful and obedient. One day I hope to join others who ran the race and did not grow weary.

Hebrews 12:1-3 reads: "Therefore, since we are surrounded by such a great cloud of witnesses, let us throw off everything that hinders and the sin that so easily entangles. And let us run with perseverance the race marked out for us, fixing our eyes on Jesus, the pioneer and perfecter of faith. For the joy set before him, he endured the cross, scorning its shame, and sat down at the right hand of the throne of God. Consider him who endured such opposition from sinners, so that you will not grow weary and lose heart."

So, why did the boy with a rare cancer die? Why was the little girl run over by a car? Why did the mother kill her little girl? Why did the tornado kill so many people? Why are people still dying today from rare conditions when we have all this technology and resources? Why?

We do not know the answers but we have to know for some reason, there is a plan. With that being said, we must also remember that we do have free will and there are some things that happen that we have caused. Too often, we take control of situations and cause more damage than good. We cannot always blame God for unwelcoming circumstances.

Stop being angry at an outcome you caused. I'm sure you've heard this phrase a time or two, "Let go, and let God." Well, it's true. Try it!

There will be times that we will suffer. The Bible reads in Romans 5:3-5: "Not only so, but we also glory in our sufferings, because we know that suffering produces perseverance; perseverance, character; and character, hope.

 And hope does not put us to shame, because God's love has been poured out into our hearts through the Holy Spirit, who has been given to us."

Reflections

Chapter 9

Nostalgia Moment

The Oxford English Dictionary defines nostalgia as... a sentimental longing for or regretful memory of a period of the past, especially one in an individual's own lifetime; (also) sentimental imagining or evocation of a period of the past.

Nostalgia is often my state of mind as I am always thinking and longing for those who have come and gone in my life.

Some left an awe-inspiring impact, and some left many traumatic memories. Each person, no matter the outcome of our relationship, have all helped to shape me into the person I am today.

On December 15, 2012, I lost the most precious, loving, caring, and near flawless woman in my life.

She taught me to have morals, to love, to have faith, and to always place God first in my life.

My Grandma Willa was the epitome of what a woman should be. I watched her many times reading her leather-bound dilapidated Bible with such sincerity and joy. As she thumbed through the crisp pages to find me a scripture about my current life situation, her voice carried strength, hope, and encouragement.

Whatever life threw at me; when I shared it with my grandma, God's Word was always in the mix.
Her life reflected this verse: "and He said to him, 'You shall love the Lord your God with all your heart and with all your soul and with all your mind." Matthew 22:37

At age 92 my Grandma Willa was still wearing high heels; not the wedge kind; the kind that are long and thin like an ink pen. She was short in stature, but not near as tall as me. I am only 4 feet 10 ½ inches tall.

 Even with her high heels on, she was short, but somehow; along the way she was given the name Big Willa.

My Grandma Willa was as tiny as a toothpick but still vigorous. When she walked into the church building, or any room for that matter, there was always a pep in each step; and your face met her face with a smile.

My memories of my Grandmother were all good. Not one recollection has ever brought me distress. She was my peace. If wishes came true, my wish would be for her to answer the phone when I call. Oh, I have so much to tell her.

Recently, I listened to a song that took me back to the days I spent with her. It goes like this, "Grandma's hands used to ache sometimes and swell, grandma's hands used to hand me a piece of candy, grandma's hands used to pray for me, when I get to heaven I will look for grandma's hands."

I will never forget the day my grandma died. It was Saturday afternoon. There I stood in the middle of Dollar General with my hands full of groceries and my phone ringing.

Normally I would let it ring until my hands were free, but this day I decided to put my stuff down and answer.

When I did, my life stood still. I yelled for my nephew who was on the other side of the store. We dropped everything and quickly went to the car. If teleporting were real, I would have wished for it to happen that day.

With trembling hands, I drove to Carbondale. I declined my nephew's offer to drive because I just knew I could get there faster but it seemed like an eternity to get there.

When we finally arrived, my face was puffy from crying the whole way there.

I was hesitant to walk into the hospital; I was not sure of what I would see.

When I entered the room, my Grandma Willa was lying so peaceful.

So many loved ones surrounded her bed… praying and crying. I thought to myself; this cannot be happening. Not her, please Lord not her. "I want my grandma." I muttered quietly.

As she lay in a coma, I watched her blood pressure drop slowly. There was nothing I could do. Nothing anyone could do. It was all in God's hands.

I am usually the strong one in my family when it comes to wanting to protect them from hurt or harm. On the day my grandma passed, I felt helpless. The most loving person we all knew, was slipping away.

I tried my best to be strong when I had to call my Dad to tell him that his Mom was not going to make it. It was the hardest thing I ever had to do.

My heart broke in a thousand pieces because I knew he had a 4-hour drive to get to her, much longer than I had. With that said, I didn't anticipate my Dad getting there in time before they pulled the plug, so I told my Dad I would put the phone to Grandma Willa's ear. It was heart-wrenching when I pulled the phone away and heard my Dad cry for the first time in my life. It broke my heart hearing him cry and utter the words "I love you Mom," for the very last time.

The doctors came in and informed us that they were about to pull the plug. I stood by my Grandma Willa's side and held her hand.

As I touched her brow, I wondered if she could sense our presence. I wanted to believe she could hear us. I looked at the leads dangling from her body. As I followed them to the monitor, I watched the numbers decline.

I will never forget watching that machine. Her blood pressure was dropping so fast. The machine finally went to zero and then it flat lined, followed by a beeping sound. As I clutched harder to my Grandma Willa's hand, it was like I could feel her slowly slipping away. At that moment, time stood still. Just like that she was gone.

Holding back the tears, I asked my cousin if she would sing "Amazing Grace."

The atmosphere was awkward with my Grandma Willa lying there lifeless. We all joined in singing Amazing Grace; it was such a comfort.

Before they came to take my Grandma Willa away, I took her ring off and gave it to my Aunt Mary, who was my Grandma Willa's only daughter.

I know my Grandma Willa could not feel anything, but as I twisted the ring on her small, cold, wrinkly hand; I thought I was hurting her. Her hands had been through so much.

The memories of her and the life she lived gives me comfort. She loved beyond limits. She was mighty even in her short stature.

My Grandma Willa was the anchor that held our family together. Her funeral, "Home Going Celebration" as we called it; lasted nearly 4 hours. Wow! What a legacy she left behind.

I loved my Grandma Willa and she loved me. Her wisdom and poise will carry on with me as well as all she knew. This verse reminds me of my Grandma Willa, Proverbs 4:23 reads: "Above all else, guard your heart, for everything you do flows from it."

I do not want you to think I am talking about my Grandma as if she was a god, because there is only one God, and He should always remain first in our lives.

My grandma was pretty special to me. Grandma Willa allowed God to live through her just as it reads in Romans 8:10: "But if Christ is in you, though the body is dead because of sin, the spirit is life because of righteousness." If I could speak to my Grandma Willa now, I would say; thank you Grandma for teaching me about God.

It took years to get out of my head the last beeps I heard as she slipped away. Every time I watch someone on a machine, that memory of my Grandma came to me. Today, I think about those beeps as time is ticking away. We have only a short time left to spend with our loved ones. Enjoy one another's company!

Reflections

_____

_____

_____

_____

_____

_____

_____

_____

_____

_____

_____

_____

_____

_____

_____

_____

_____

_____

Chapter 10

In His Image

I've heard so many people say, they are ugly and hate getting their picture taken. My response is usually, well you do not walk around with a mirror in front of you all day looking at yourself. I see you, and I see a beautiful person. The way you perceive yourself is not always, how others see you.

Stop insulting yourself!

When I was younger, there was a time when I hid from the camera. I hated getting my picture taken.

Today, I can "selfie" all day long. Maybe when I was younger I had lower self-esteem.

When we have low self-esteem, often we do not feel pretty. Whatever has caused us to feel this way, whether it be our weight, bad hair day, emotional abuse, physical abuse, pimples, ugly scars, or depression; we must conquer it with loving ourselves and confidence.

Loving yourself is the big key here. You have to love who you are in order to love what you see. My face isn't flawless and I'm for sure not the typical size model, but I love who I am - my smile, my compassion, my God-given talents, my sparkling eyes, my chubby cheeks, and so much more that's unique about me.

When I focus more on the fact that I am created in the image of God, nothing else matters. Genesis 1:27 reads: "So God created mankind in his own image, in the image of God he created them; male and female he created them."

None of us are perfect. Not even a typical size model. We all have flaws. The body I live in is a temporary tent that God gave me.

1 Corinthians 6:19-20 reads: "Do you not know that your bodies are temples of the Holy Spirit, who is in you, whom you have received from God? You are not your own;

you were bought at a price. Therefore, honor God with your bodies."

One day my body will waste away and all I want people to remember about me, was the life I lived and who I was as a person. Not, "Oh wasn't her nose just perfect?" or "Didn't she have the cutest eyelashes?"

God's word says to offer our bodies as a living sacrifice. Romans 12:1-2 reads: "Therefore, I urge you, brothers and sisters, in view of God's mercy, to offer your bodies as a living sacrifice, holy and pleasing to God—this is your true and proper worship. Do not conform to the pattern of this world, but be transformed by the renewing of your mind. Then you will be able to test and approve what God's will is—his good, pleasing and perfect will."

How I present myself to others should be what matters most, not what shade of lipstick I'm wearing or the latest fashionable clothing.

I get it, low self-esteem isn't something you can turn on and off like a light switch. It takes work and most of all a desire to want to be set free from self-destruction.

Can you be a Christian and have low self-esteem? Yes, but you should want to do something about it and meditate on God's Word.

Do not stay in that rut!

You know as a Christian the Holy Spirit is already a resident in your life. You invited him in so act like it! If half of us spent more time worrying about the inside rather than the outside, we might see some changes in how we view ourselves.

Take a moment and look at yourself in the mirror. Tell yourself, "Self, I am created in the image of God; I have the Holy Spirit within me; God has designed me just the way that I am; I am beautiful; I am a child of God."

Own it, claim it, and live it!

As a society, we have to stop thinking about what others think about us and be more concerned about the life we live as "Christians."

The Bible says to study to show thou self-approved, and not ashamed.

2 Timothy 2:15 reads: "Be diligent to present yourself approved to God, a worker who does not need to be ashamed, rightly dividing the word of truth."

Studying God's Word empowers us to know how to live and what our destiny will be if we remain faithful until the end.

Do you see where I'm going with this? It's not what others say that should matter, it's what God's Word says. Remember, He created us, not man. My creator didn't create junk.

When I feel discouraged or start to have self-pity for whatever reason, I like to turn to the verse in Psalm 51:10: "Create in me a pure heart, O God, and renew a steadfast spirit within me."

The awesomeness of God's Word erases all the ugliness I feel.

Try it!

Turn to His Word and apply it to your life. What you put into your life will come out of your life. If you do not feel connected to God or you're not seeking to be pleasing in his sight, you need to fix it.

When a person constantly complains about their life and stressors but does nothing about it, then the song gets old. Don't get me wrong, God never gets tired of hearing your woes, He loves us, but He does want us to make a change and put Him first.

Mark 12:30- 31 reads: "Love the Lord your God with all your heart and with all your soul and with all your mind and with all your strength." The second is this: "Love your neighbor as yourself." There is no commandment greater than these."

Wow! Love your neighbor as you love yourself. This would be difficult if you don't love yourself.

The Bible says in Ephesians 5:29 reads: "For no one has ever hated his own body, but he nourishes and tenderly cares for it, as the Messiah does the church."

Those words should radiate through your life. Another verse about loving yourself is in Proverbs 19:8, "To acquire wisdom is to love oneself; people who cherish understanding will prosper."

Don't beat yourself up over the simple things. Believe in yourself and always remember it's the He in you that makes all the difference.

This next verse speaks for itself in Romans 5:8, "But God commendeth his love toward us, in that, while we were yet sinners, Christ died for us."

Christ died for me. Yes, this girl with a slight astigmatism in one eye, chubby cheeks, and a round and pudgy nose. I am still important to God. No matter what I feel about my outside appearance; I must first love who I am and instill Gods Words into every ounce of my being.

Next time, smile at the camera with boldness and confidence. Remember, the Holy Spirit is shining through you.

Reflections

_____

_____

_____

_____

_____

_____

_____

_____

_____

_____

_____

_____

_____

_____

_____

_____

_____

Chapter 11

He Will Wipe Every Tear

I begin this with great sadness in my heart, after hearing the news of a young man who committed suicide in my community.

 The community searched for hours to find this young man after he had posted a Facebook suicide note. The note was very descriptive and it was obvious he did not want to be found right away.

As the day grew longer, I clung on to hope that they would find him in time.

Search parties were forming and the plea for any of his whereabouts was growing with desperation. While all of this is taking place, his little girl had no idea what was going on, or where her daddy was.

This young man saw freeing himself from pain was better for himself, but it only caused pain to his loved ones. His little girl is now left to wonder why her daddy killed himself.

This brings me to say, if you are hurting or know anyone hurting, do not ignore it. There is so much that we have to be thankful for, but I know the pain can cloud our judgement.

I'm sure this family must have asked; why didn't I know? What could I have said to change his mind? Why didn't he come to me? What did I do to cause this for him? The list could go on. No one may be to blame, all we do know is that this man was hurting so bad that nothing in life "at that moment" mattered.

Life's issues will always define us, but we do not have to let it overshadow our worth. If you are going through a tough time and the light at the end of the tunnel is no longer shining, please, do not give up.

The light is only dim for a short while. If you just hold on a little longer, you will see a ray of hope and people who love you there to help you through.

I like the verse in 2 Corinthians 4:17-18; "For our light and momentary troubles are achieving for us an eternal glory that far outweighs them all. So, we fix our eyes not on what is seen, but on what is unseen, since what is seen is temporary, but what is unseen is eternal."

Temporary is the keyword. When I am going through a tough time, I have to remind myself; "this too shall pass."

Does it seem evident at that time? More than likely no, but there is always another day.

Do you recall the book of Job? A man who stood upright and blameless but faced a life of harshness stricken with much sorrow. Job lost his children, livestock, harvest, and his strength. Job 6:11 reads: "What strength do I have, that I should still hope? What prospects, that I should be patient?"

There are many people like Job out there. Some may feel defeated and want to throw in the towel. I am sure Job may have felt that way a time or two. I know I would have.

The lesson we can learn from Job is: remain faithful to God even through the test of hard times.

When life feels like it is falling apart and you have lost your strength and hope, do not stop praising God. Job did not forsake God. He clung to Him more.

As a Christian, I can say the hope I find through each day is in my Lord and Savior. However, what if you are not a Christian and none of this makes sense to you.

Maybe you're not anything like Job and your situation is totally different.

Whatever the case; this stands true; God loves us all. He will give us comfort and the will to go on if we turn our lives to Him. God's Word states clearly in James 1:6: "that we must believe and not doubt."

I wish the young man that took his life would have believed there was hope if he would have just held on a little longer.

Is something bothering you? Are your bills past due? Does your husband/wife not look at you the same way as they did when you first met? Are your children caught up in the law? Did you lose a job? Are you addicted to something that is ruling and controlling your life? Are you depressed? Are you feeling hopeless? Do you feel worthless? Is your will to live shadowed with despair?

Keep holding on! Do not give up because TODAY seems gloomy, there is always tomorrow.

Count your blessings!

One day, when the Lord calls home all those who have believed and remained faithful until the end; it will all be worth the struggles you endured for this short time.

Revelation 21:4 reads: "He will wipe every tear from their eyes. There will be no more death or mourning or crying o pain, for the old order of things has passed away."

Reflections

_____

_____

_____

_____

_____

_____

_____

_____

_____

_____

_____

_____

_____

_____

_____

_____

_____

Chapter 12

A New Day

"This is the day that the Lord has made, let us rejoice and be glad in it." (Psalm 118:24). This verse should get us excited to live, love, and share God's Word with others.

When I was going through some rough patches; people used to say, "Tomorrow is a brand-new day." Well at the time, those words didn't seem too encouraging.

Sometimes we get so overwhelmed with life's demanding agendas, work, deadlines, college exams, household chores, and so much more; that a new day is just the same as any other day.

Try to change your way of thinking when a new day comes. Greet your new day with a positive attitude and a goal to make it better than yesterday.

If you dwell on yesterday, then you rob today of any chance of a fresh new start.

Point is... no matter how you wake up to today, it will always be a new day. The rest is up to you.

It would sound silly to say; "It's a new day so that bill you were worrying about yesterday, forget about it." That's not what I'm saying.

As I said earlier there are just some things we can't change and it will roll over into each new day we are blessed to see. If we adjust our attitude with hopes of having a better day today than yesterday, it will not make the bill go away, but it will confirm that the world didn't crumble just because of that overdue bill.

Take the proper steps needed to figure it out and then move on.

What if it's a sickness you're dealing with instead of a bill? It's a new day, right? You are still sick or suffering from a chronic illness. You wonder what now? How will today be any better than yesterday?

First, you made it another day. Second, you have a chance to be an inspiration to someone else.

Thirdly, you now have confidence in knowing that the Lord will guide, lead and direct you throughout any day, when you put on His full armor.

Stand firm today and suit up! Strap on the belt of truth which is Jesus Christ; protect yourself with the breastplate of righteousness; hold before you the shield of faith, that you may block the flaming arrows of evil that will try and detour you today, put on the helmet of salvation, believe that you belong to one who will protect you and lastly, hold firmly to the sword of the spirit which is the Word of God. (Paraphrased from Ephesians 6:8-10).

Daily we fight battles that others don't even know we are fighting. Not everyone can gracefully enter a new day with excitement.

As Christians, we can rest assured that the Lord will continue to equip us with the tools needed to guard us through those tough days.

One of the biggest mistakes made is starting a new day by adding God last. Start each morning by thanking the Lord for blessing you.

Pray that you will have the strength needed to make it through the day. Rely on God's Word to give you hope, peace, and direction.

I used to work at a place where I dreaded going in each day. I knew I was going to a place where edification didn't even exist. Words of encouragement were few.

My attitude as a Christian became challenging as I entered the building and wanted to ignore everyone. A new day to me became a day of doom and gloom.

One day I decided to stop putting the Lord last. I woke up, prayed, prayed again in the parking lot, and walked in suited in my armor. Work changed for me. My days were filled with a little more joy. Try it!

Reflections

_____

_____

_____

_____

_____

_____

_____

_____

_____

_____

_____

_____

_____

_____

_____

_____

_____

_____

Chapter 13

Deeply Rooted

Like a tree that's deeply rooted, I too want to be rooted in God's Word.

We know that the roots of a tree are the foundation. Without deep roots, the tree cannot stand. There are times when a bad storm comes along and the roots can no longer hold, causing the tree to fall.

I want to be grounded in God's Word no matter what tries to knock me over.

The world we live in is full of heartaches. Don't be knocked over with doubt but trust the thought that life will get better. Stay grounded!

If we read God's Word and make it our foundation, then there is hope in knowing that there are better days to come.

I've seen trees cut down but the trunk was left deeply rooted.

When you are having a difficult time and feel like your surroundings are crushing you, do not give in. Remember the foundation on which you stand.

If there is one thing I have learned studying God's Word... it will not return to me empty.

Isaiah 55:11 reads: "So, shall My word be that goes forth from My mouth; It shall not return to Me [a]void, but it shall accomplish what I please, and it shall prosper in the thing for which I sent it."

Over the years I've read a lot of books, and articles. Some aren't worth reading again and some left me confused and empty.

Now do not get me wrong, reading is good and I love books. I actually turned one of my rooms into a library.

The point I'm making is, most of the books are fiction. Not any facts in them at all. The Bible is far from that.

While some may believe that the Bible is a fantasy book written by men that were delusional, I do not believe that.

The Bible is God inspired. It is the truth and reality. I do not need to try and convince you, just look around. Even with all the ugliness in this world, someone gave birth to a beautiful baby while you are reading this. Someone who has been searching for years, finally is reunited with their family. Storms may have come and destroyed cities, but look now... look at the growth not only in material things but in the unity of a community.

We need to be a people that abides in God's Word. You will find freedom in the truth. John 8:31-32 reads: "to those Jews who believed Him, "If you abide in My word, you are

My disciples indeed. And you shall know the truth, and the truth shall make you free."

Look at the tree in the picture on page 100. Do you see how it leans to the side as if it's about to give at any time?

It hasn't yet and it's been that way for a long time. Maybe it's time we stop doubting our strength in the Lord and re-examine our foundation.

Luke 6:48 reads: "He is like a man building a house, who dug deep and laid the foundation on the rock. And when the flood arose, the stream beat vehemently against that house, and could not shake it, for it was founded on the rock."

If you are looking for truth, understanding, and hope in something more grounded than where you've been, get deeply rooted in God's Word.

Reflections

_____

_____

_____

_____

_____

_____

_____

_____

_____

_____

_____

_____

_____

_____

_____

_____

_____

_____

_____

Chapter 14

Standing in your own way

Do you feel like your blessings are blocked? Maybe you can't understand why today has been the worst day of your life. So, it seems that way. Every mountain you've tried to climb today left you flat on your back in the lowest valley.

You are frustrated, mad, and ready to point a finger at who or what has caused your abysmal kind of day.

Before you go on a fault-finding rant, evaluate your attitude. Were you nice to the person standing in front of you at the store? How about when you passed someone going down the road in a hurry? When you left home, did you leave with a smile and ready to start the day with a positive attitude?

Better yet, did you pray before leaving and ask the Lord to send you out with a Godly attitude?

If you have answered no to at least one of these questions, you are probably standing in your own way.

Yep, it's YOU! Time to fix what's causing you to have such a bad day. Yes, sometimes it can be the other person and no matter what you do to prepare yourself; nothing works. I too have been there. I went into work with a smile and nearly left in tears.

Why would I allow something I simply could not change to cause me to have such a bad attitude for the rest of the day? It uses more energy for me to frown and fret then it did to smile and pray.

There are times when I have to say to myself: "Self, I need you to get out of the way."

When we allow God to take control of our mood and outlook on life, we are better apt to have a good day.

Remember that to live a life that's pleasing to God we have to surrender even our attitude.

What if you are at work and causing all kinds of trouble but you profess to be a Christian? Yes, I said profess, because saying you are but acting like you're not, can often reflect two different things.

Are you an effective Christian? Do your speech and conversations amplify God? Do you set yourself on a pedestal and forget to give God credit for blessing you? Did you make plans to attend something you weren't comfortable with just so you could fit in?

How about this one? Around your family... do you try to shine for God? Can they see the love of Christ in you and witness a life lived by Christ's example? I can vouch for this, it is hard sometimes to do this when you have family that brings out the worst in you. My advice is, always seek peace, even if it means separation from strife.

Is some of this applying to you right now?

As a Christian, you have to put away old ways. In Ephesians 4:22 it reads: "that you put off, concerning your former conduct, the old man which grows corrupt according to the deceitful lusts."

I can't express this enough, no one is perfect, but you can pray for God to help you become a better person today than you were yesterday.

Today we live in a media world. Social Media to be exact. We've gotten away from turning to prayer and Gods Word when we are hurt, angry, or just mad at the world.

Facebook is not your savior. It is not going to give you anything but grief and something you can't take back later when you get involved with venting your feelings to the world out of anger. Once those evil, degrading, mean, bad tempered words leave your mouth and travel to your fingertips onto the keyboard and then into the cyber world, that's it.

Sure, you can retract and delete it and hope you did soon enough, but chances are they already had 100 views.

Did you think to pray before you took to social media? Try asking God to help you deal with whatever it was before you send it off into the cyber world.

Let me share some scriptures to help you next time you explode with anger before thinking.

"Let no corrupt word proceed out of your mouth, but what is good for necessary edification, that it may impart grace to the hearers." (Ephesians 4:29)

"Not what goes into the mouth defiles a man; but what comes out of the mouth, this defiles a man." (Matthew 15:11)

"Set a guard, O Lord, over my mouth; Keep watch over the door of my lips." (Psalm 141:3)

"He who has knowledge spares his words, and a man of understanding is of a calm spirit." (Proverbs 17:27)

"A soft answer turns away wrath, but a harsh word stirs up anger." (Proverbs 15:1)

Reflections

_____
_____
_____
_____
_____
_____
_____
_____
_____
_____
_____
_____
_____
_____
_____
_____
_____
_____

Gone yet
not forgotten,
...ugh we are apart,
...our spirit lives
within me,
...rever in my hea...

Chapter 15

A Christian for Christ

I spoke a little about being an ambassador in one of the other chapters. Being an ambassador for Christ really means something to me. To be an ambassador for Christ, my life must match what is pleasing in His sight. It is my duty as a Christian to amplify the love of Christ and His Word.

If I am not living my life to match what I stand for in Christ, then how can I be a good influence to those around me?

Sometimes we get so wrapped up in the words "I am a Christian," that we forget what the job of a Christian is.

Being a Christian doesn't give us more privileges than it does others. It doesn't give us the authority to belittle others or judge those who are out of the will of God.

Being a Christian comes with great sacrifices. It's not about us but the He that is in us.

The duties of a Christian are, always to first and foremost, strive to learn God's precious Word and share it with others. "We must also share the word with others while planting seeds of encouragement." (2 Timothy 2:15).

When is the last time you shared God's Word with someone? Even smiling at the person next to you and share how good God is can plant a seed.

We do not have to beat them on the head with a Bible or give a sermon that tears them apart for all the wrongs in their life. Just share the love of Christ and be humble.

The sympathy we have for those who are not living in the will of God, should transform into empathy because we once stood where they did. Our lives have not always been perfect and never will be.

Romans 6:6 reads: "For we know that our old self was crucified with him so that the body ruled by sin might be done away with, that we should no longer be slaves to sin."

Yes, we are human but with that said we have an obligation as Christians to love, live, and shine for Christ.

When we became Christians, we became a chosen people. 1 Peter 2:9 reads: "But you are a chosen people, a royal priesthood, a holy nation, God's special possession, that you may declare the praises of him who called you out of darkness into his wonderful light."

This scripture inspires me. To know that I am God's special possession gives me the confidence in living boldly for Him. I am a Christian for Christ. Are you a Christian for Christ?

It is difficult sometimes to share the Word of God in places such as work, meetings, schools, and with some family members.

No matter the atmosphere, let your light shine. People are always watching everything you say and do. Your ways are a testament to who you profess to be.

At work I may not can talk to others about God, but I can live in a manner that they see Him in me.

I do not engage in conversations that are filthy, vulgar, or degrading. I do not laugh at jokes that tear another person down. I do not jump on board the "insult train" when someone points a finger at someone else. I am a Christian for Christ.

As I said previously, there is more to just saying, "I am a Christian." Live like it. Be it 24/7. Turn from things that do not lift one another up and amplify Christ.

This chapter is not to point a finger at you; it is to let you know that we have a duty as Christians.

We have to be more forthcoming. Our voices need to ring out about what the Bible says.

Stop going along with the popular, and acceptable way of life. Always stand firm in the word.

Ephesians 6:11 reads: "Put on the full armor of God, so that you can take your stand against the devil's schemes."

Unbelievably, the devil schemes are all around us. At work, in our families, at school, public functions, and even a battle within ourselves.

Proverbs 3:5-6 reads: "Trust in the Lord with all your heart and lean not on your own understanding; in all your ways submit to him, and he will make your paths straight."

Reflections

_____

_____

_____

_____

_____

_____

_____

_____

_____

_____

_____

_____

_____

_____

_____

Chapter 16

Weeping may endure for a night

I have always heard this verse growing up, "For his anger lasts only a moment, but his favor lasts a lifetime; weeping may stay for the night, but rejoicing comes in the morning." (Psalm 30:5).

Most of the time it was when someone had died. It was to remind those grieving that our sadness here on earth was joy for those who went to the other side.

Recently my friend lost her husband. He was a good man. A man whose life was a model after Christ. I silently grieved over his loss. I was thinking more of the sadness my friend had and the emptiness she would have going forward.

My days were shadowed with grief and disbelief that he was really gone. My thoughts were, this cannot be happening. What will his wife do now? What will I do knowing this man's wisdom carried me through some things in my own life?

Even though I knew the loss would be difficult, the comfort I found was that I knew he was in a better place.

Grief has many stages. To name a few: denial, isolation, anger, bargaining, acceptance, and depression. These stages are the psychological way of dealing with a loss. Each person will grieve in his or her own time and some will not be able to come to terms with life after a loss.

It is ok to grieve. The sorrow we feel after a loss is often indescribable. Our hearts ache and we feel such an emptiness. Do not be ashamed to share what you feel. Sharing can be a great outlet.

I too have suffered losses that nearly tore my heart out. I went through so many stages that I cannot even explain.

Some days it seemed like life was going on without me mentally being there. I felt lifeless! I began to think of how Jesus felt when his friend Lazarus died. John 11:35 is one of the shortest verses in the Bible: "Jesus wept." Was he weeping for the loss of his friend?

We know Jesus had the power to raise him again. I believe that he wept also for the ones left behind that were weeping. Jesus compassion even in his loss were for others. What a comfort to have someone by our side to help us through this suffering… Matthew 5:4 reads: "Blessed are those who mourn, for they will be comforted."

As a Christian what a comfort to know that those who remained faithful to the Lord will one day be joined with him and all those gone on before. I would love to see my Grandma again someday. I am sure my friend's husband is now on the other side with those he loved… singing and shouting with joy.

Grief is a journey we all will take. When my sister died, it was hard riding in the big black car during the procession. You know the car for the family that leads the body to its final resting place. As I sat in that car, I looked out the window at all the bystanders. People pulled over to the side of the road, just as they should out of respect. Some I could see in their eyes as they were sad for my loss.

That feeling of knowing I may never see my sister again, made my insides turn. I was overwhelmed with grief.

Today, nearly 14 years later I am not where I was. Yes, my heart still aches and I am saddened around remembrance days, such as, her birthday, or the day she died. I am able to lift my head a little higher as the years go on, but it's still painful to knowing she's not here with us.

If you are suffering from a loss, find comfort in the Lord. You are not alone. Reach out to friends and other family members.

It's not good to keep everything bottled up inside. Find someone to talk too. Do not be afraid to cry on someone's shoulder. Your journey of grief is normal.

Hang tough!

Reflections

Chapter 17

Hope In Heaven

During worship service, the preacher spoke about motion with emotions. He expressed some people base their faith on what they feel and not what the Bible says.

We all get emotional from time to time. Life circumstances can cause us to respond in a sad or happy way. Reading God's Word should also stir an emotion in us.

The scripture should cause us to yearn for more.

God's Word will give you direction, hope, discipline, and joy. Each day we wake up to a new day that's filled with life's challenges. It's hard to see past the destruction in this world. Political fights are constant, homelessness is heartbreaking, and there are violent crimes every day.

As a Christian we have hope in a better place one day. We know where our eternal home is. Our duty is to share with others, so that they too can one day have a home in heaven.

Dying is a part of life. After all, we were born to one day die. The life you live in between that, is your free will. The life after that, is your free will also. Just because you have not known anyone to come back and tell you that heaven is real, doesn't mean you give up hope.

If you are reading this book, and you have never made a commitment to become a Christian, I want to encourage you to seek God's Word. His plan for salvation is free to all. He died for all, therefore, you are just as important to become a Christian as I am.

Find a Bible believing church home. One that believes from scripture, that baptism is essential for salvation. Jesus set that example for us.

Matthew 3:13- 17 reads: "Then Jesus came from Galilee to the Jordan to be baptized by John.

But John tried to deter him, saying, "I need to be baptized by you, and do you come to me?" Jesus replied, "Let it be so now; it is proper for us to do this to fulfill all righteousness." Then John consented. As soon as Jesus was baptized, he went up out of the water. At that moment heaven was opened, and he saw the Spirit of God descending like a dove and alighting on him. And a voice from heaven said, "This is my Son, whom I love; with him I am well pleased."

Before Jesus began his ministry, He knew the most important thing to do, was to be baptized.

What is keeping you from taking the next step to live for God? No one said you had to get right before you can be right. The work in you will begin when you work on you.

This place we now call home, is a temporary dwelling place. At the end of this world there will only be one of two places that will be our final home.

Heaven or hell? Enter the gates paved with gold and free from pain and suffering, or enter the gates of fire and gnashing of teeth. I can only pray that one would want to live a life that is pleasing to God. God's promises are for us to one day join Him in heaven.

John 3:16 reads: "For God so loved the world, that He gave His only begotten Son, that whosoever believes in Him, shall not perish, but have eternal life."

Reflections

_____
_____
_____
_____
_____
_____
_____
_____
_____
_____
_____
_____
_____
_____
_____
_____
_____
_____
_____

Chapter 18

Encouragement

- ♥ Do your best and let God handle the rest!

- ♥ Look around and count your blessings!

- ♥ Perfect doesn't exist, but doing what is pleasing in God's sight does!

- ♥ Hang in there, trust in the Lord!

- ♥ Trials may come your way. They will go away.

- ♥ Love and laughter will keep you sane!

- ♥ When you feel like you're drowning in life's problems, take them to God!

- ♥ You are the seed that others may need planted in their lives!

- ♥ We can't create problems and expect joy!

- ♥ Your strength can become success when you rise up!

- ♥ Having a tug-a-war with life's problems; let God's Word help you win!

- ♥ You have free will, do good things!

- ♥ If you feel defeated, read Job, he survived!

- ♥ Sickness is misery but God's promises are the best medicine!

- ♥ You can guard your heart from getting hurt, but don't guard it so much that you don't let others in to show you love!

- ♥ When you can't see the good in this world pray!

- ♥ Sadness becomes temporary when you see someone else's struggles!

- ♥ Weakness only comes when you stop acknowledging your strengths!

Made in the USA
Coppell, TX
29 September 2023

22154143R00079